WHEN I WANT TO WRITE A LOVE POEM

EMBER BIRCHALL

Copyright © 2024 Ember Birchall

All rights reserved.

ISBN: 9798862963410

I don't really know who to dedicate this book to, so I suppose if you recognise yourself in my words, then it's for you.

CONTENTS

1	The Multi-Instrumentalist	Pg 1
2	I Want to Write Him Poetry	Pg 5
3	The Day We Met	Pg 6
4	Good Morning –	Pg 7
5	The Boy I Told the Others Not to Worry About	Pg 8
6	Crush	Pg 9
7	I Was Always the Shy Girl	Pg 10
8	First Kiss	Pg 11
9	Jolene	Pg 15
10	Our Unidentifiable First Date	Pg 16
11	It Was Raining	Pg 17
12	Sitting By the Water	Pg 18
13	The First Time You Spent the Night	Pg 19
14	Did I Ever Tell You About My Sad Guitar?	Pg 20
15	Sad Guitars in August	Pg 21
16	Our Unspoken Vow	Pg 25
17	I Think It's His Eyes	Pg 26

WHEN I WANT TO WRITE A LOVE POEM

18	In The Dark	Pg 27
19	An Unrequited Love Affair	Pg 28
20	Passenger Seat	Pg 29
21	Haven't Spoken For Months	Pg 30
22	Unattached	Pg 31
23	Tattoos & Temptation	Pg 32
24	IX XII XXI	Pg 33
25	The Night After	Pg 34
26	Late Night Conversations	Pg 35
27	Bad Habits	Pg 36
28	When I Want to Write a Love Poem	Pg 37
29	I Wish You Came With A Warning	Pg 38
30	Truth Or Dare?	Pg 39
31	The Night She Was There	Pg 43
32	The First Violin	Pg 44
33	Secret Symphony	Pg 45
34	No More Scattered Nights, please?	Pg 46
35	Home By Midnight	Pg 47
36	A Different Kind of Adrenaline	Pg 48
37	What Would We Be Like?	Pg 49
38	Grand Piano	Pg 50
39	He Liked My Poetry	Pg 51

40	The Day I Saw You in Town with Her	Pg 52
41	Their Song	Pg 55
42	When You Read My Poetry	Pg 56
43	I Still Have the Bottle of Vodka	Pg 57
44	We Were Never Romeo & Juliet	Pg 58
45	One Last Night	Pg 59
46	We Were Gonna Be Timeless	Pg 60
47	Last Kiss	Pg 61
48	Message Not Delivered	Pg 62
49	A Poet in Love	Pg 64
50	When I Want to Write a Love Poem (Reprised)	Pg 65
51	The Highs & Lows of Heartbreak	Pg 69
52	Pinterest Boards & Nursery Walls	Pg 70
53	Dancing On My Own	Pg 71
54	Do Your Symphonies Sound Like Ours?	Pg 72
55	You'll Be Crying Over Me	Pg 73
56	Losing You	Pg 74
57	Loving Myself	Pg 75
58	Progress	Pg 76
59	I Don't Love You	Pg 77
60	Goodbye Sad Guitar	Pg 78

THE MULTI-INSTRUMENTALIST

I am the multi-instrumentalist – a one person band. I parade my way through this world making as much noise as possible with as many instruments as I can. I've played sad guitars, took classes on how to make piano keys sing, played the saxophone until the early hours of the night – I've even learned to play a harmonica and a violin at the same time. But I've also been that sad guitar. I've been made to sing like piano keys, been compelled to sing by saxophones, been played by a harmonica and violin together. I've been judged and bullied for not choosing an instrument for the class band because I can't decide between drums and an electric base – but there was once a time when I was afraid of the music – a time when I lived in complete silence. But then I picked up my first sad guitar – my first violin, and I found a way to make them sing. They found a way to make me sing and suddenly I wasn't so afraid anymore.

WHEN I WANT TO WRITE A LOVE POEM

AQUAINTANCES

WHEN I WANT TO WRITE A LOVE POEM

I WANT TO WRITE HIM POETRY

I want to write him poetry – I want to write him lyrics that he can play on his guitar when he's alone under the stars. Whenever he strums the strings – when his fingers mold to new chords, I want him to think of me. I want him to think of the night when we created our own genres as we experimented between the sheets or the time we went for a late-night drive. Sometimes I want to ask him if he still thinks about that night, if he remembers the way our lips pressed together or the way I melted into his embrace, but even after he made me shake like thunder – I'm still too shy.

THE DAY WE MET

I wanted to write a poem about the
first time we met, but as I sit here
staring at the empty page and thinking
back over the years, I realise that I
don't actually remember it. I can
remember everything else, the times
we'd spend in the milkshake bar,
that your favourite flavour was mentos,
or that your favourite video game is
Cave Story, but I can't remember the
first day we met – our first conversation.
I assume it was in a classroom, surrounded
by grey and other lifeless students,
decorated with colourful ties of blue,
purple and gold, in a building built on
broken promises and bribery of false
futures. I was probably asking you to
dumb down whatever computerised
jargon the teacher was shouting at us. It
might have been the day we first started
looking at python, I probably cried
because of the gibberish on my screen.
I don't remember the first day we met,
but I imagine it went something like that.

GOOD MORNING –

I used to send you a text every day
to say good morning, do you remember?
I'd call you the name that you deemed
to be ironic despite my constant denial. I
used to text you every morning without
fail, she hated it – but I wasn't going to
stop just to make her comfortable, I wasn't
going to ignore your sad face just to keep
her happy. It's sad that she never seemed
to understand that that's all it was, just
a text to say good morning, nothing more,
nothing less, if she did, then we probably
could have been friends. Not the kind to
endure sleepovers and tell each other
everything, but she would have hated my
existence less if she didn't jump to conclusions.

THE BOY I TOLD THE OTHERS NOT TO WORRY ABOUT

In the early days you were the boy
that I always told the others not to worry
about. Every girl has that one male friend
that their boyfriend is always suspicious
of, and for me – that was you. Yours
was the name that would always trigger
raised eyebrows, judgmental side-eyes and
sarcastic comments, but I could never see
it. You were the friend I'd vent to on bad
days or who I'd go to looking for advice
when there was a guy, I was trying to impress,
but then we kissed that day over the Christmas
holidays and my whole world view changed.

CRUSH

Like Hazel's love for Augustus, I
developed a crush on you in the same
way that I fall asleep – slowly at first,
and then all at once. But I'll always deny
it because you see – admitting it would
be like admitting defeat, and why would
I want to do that? It would be like admitting
that I felt something during that moment
of madness that became the reason I smile
whenever I hear Fairytale of New York.
No – I could never admit to anything. It
could ruin everything if I did.

I WAS ALWAYS THE SHY GIRL

"SOMETIMES I WISH SOMEONE OUT THERE WILL
FIND ME, 'TIL THEN I WALK ALONE."
- BOULEVARD OF BROKEN DREAMS, GREEN DAY

Before you came along – I was
always the shy girl. Too shy to speak,
to breathe, to even exist, when I told
my friend that I liked you, I regretted
that life choice instantly as she teased
me incessantly for days on end until I tried
to pluck up the courage to as you out on
a date. You might even remember that day
of my failed attempt as I forgot to mention
that it was a date and your friend who
was with you invited himself along. I grew
so overwhelmed that I forgot to even mention
a time or a place. I ended up spending that
Saturday alone sitting in a coffee shop in town
looking through the window trying to find
you in the crowd and then ducking down to
hide when I saw your friend walk by.

FIRST KISS

"SINATRA WAS SINGING, ALL THE DRUNKS THEY
WERE SWINGING. WE KISSED ON THE CORNER THEN
DANCED THROUGH THE NIGHT."
- FAIRYTALE OF NEW YORK, THE POGUES FEAT.
KIRSTY MACCOLL

As far as first kisses go, yours is one
of the few that I still think about. Do
you remember that day? We'd just been
roller skating with a group of friends,
and you were waiting in the bus station
with me for my bus back to my dad's
house. It's a day that I'll never forget. It's
a day I don't want to forget. Now years
later whenever I'm sitting on that bench
waiting for my bus home, I think about the
way your fingers felt in my hair and the
way your lips tasted when pressed against
mine. We've both come such a long way
since then, we barely see each other anymore
but when we do meet it feels like no time
has passed. Do you feel that way? Some days
I feel like I don't want to know, I'd rather
live in false hope than know for certain, but
then curiosity creeps in and I find myself
awake late at night writing poems where
I ask you for answers.

WHEN I WANT TO WRITE A LOVE POEM

BUILD-UP

WHEN I WANT TO WRITE A LOVE POEM

JOLENE

She called me Jolene that day
we went to the cinema. I know I
shouldn't have laughed but I
couldn't help myself. I didn't plan
this. I didn't plan you. It just happened –
we just happened. I wanted to point
out that I don't have eyes of emerald
green or that you left of your own
free will – but there was nothing
that I could say for her to see sense.
Whenever that song plays on the
radio or on my CDs at the caravan, I
picture her face on the bus that day.

OUR UNIDENTIFABLE FIRST DATE

We never ended up having a first date, there was never a time when it was just us two. Sure, we went roller skating or out for drinks, but it was usually with a group of friends – it never felt like there was a day when it was just us – except for that one time. Do you remember it? I don't remember all of it, just the part where I got stuck in a kid's car ride and you couldn't help me for laughing before taking the opportunity to run off with my cans. I still haven't forgiven you for that, even if it was years ago. We should do that again, some time. After our kiss over the holidays I was scared it was going to be awkward, but it ended up being one of my favourite days.

IT WAS RAINING

It was raining that day on the
swings, kind of like it is today. As
I sit here listening to the pitter
patter of raindrops on the roof,
I think about that day when it rained,
and the sky was alive with hailstone.
We were freezing but I wasn't ready
to go home yet – I don't think you
were either. So, we stayed and kissed
in the rain like all those old movies
said that we should.

SITTING BY THE WATER

"I REMEMBER HOW IT FELT SITTING BY THE WATER, AND EVERY TIME I LOOK AT YOU, IS LIKE THE FIRST TIME."
- MINE (TAYLOR'S VERSION), TAYLOR SWIFT

On days when life is hard to take,
I think about that bank holiday Monday
when we went to the beach. I can still
remember the way the sand felt beneath
our feet and the cold spray of the sea
when we stood too close to the waves.
Despite everything we were still so shy
around each other. Did you ever notice
that it was exactly a year later when we
went to the beach again? I still have
our selfie together somewhere as we sat
on the pebbles getting sprayed by the sea.

THE FIRST TIME YOU SPENT THE NIGHT

I remember I was nervous the first time you spent the night. I'd cleared out the spare room for you to sleep in there but it ended up being a wasted task as we fell asleep together in my bed after watching movies on my laptop. We stayed up all night talking and fell asleep with your arms wrapped tight around me. Can we do that again? No music, no lightning, not even quiet thunder, just us lying together in the dark with a movie playing quietly in the background. We're both too busy for that now – we both had to grow up. But it would be nice.

DID I EVER TELL YOU ABOUT MY SAD GUITAR?

Did I ever tell you about my sad
guitar? He was one of the good ones.
He was and still is someone I know
I can turn to on a bad day. Even on
days when he can only think in a minor
key, I know that in one way or another,
he'll be there when it's important. I
call him my sad guitar because he had
a special skill for making a lament out
of a celebration, but despite this, I've
been able to cry tears of laughter because
of him. On a good day, we will laugh
and smile, drink and be happy recalling
the time we were chased by cattle or the
time we got lost in Lymm Dam, those
were the good days. In a weird way, when
people ask, I credit him for making me
the person who I am today. Whether
that's a good thing or a bad thing I'll
let you decide, but because of his reassurance
and whispers late at night, I'm no longer
ashamed of my scars, he made a rebel of
a careless man's careful daughter. He's one
of the best things that's ever been mine.

SAD GUITARS IN AUGUST

"HE MADE A REBEL OF A CARELESS MANS, CAREFUL DAUGHTER. HE IS THE BEST THING, THAT'S EVER BEEN MINE."
- MINE (TAYLOR'S VERSION), TAYLOR SWIFT.

I played my first sad guitar on an
August afternoon, the summer sun was
beating down and breaking in through
the bedroom window – I never expected
to hear the strings singing, not with him.
Not that day. When I was younger and
imagining my first concert, I thought I
knew who it would be – I thought I knew
the music that would be played – but I'm
glad that it was him. I'm glad that he
was my first sad guitar. I never told him
that – that I'm glad that he was the first
song that I learned to play on that August
afternoon. I suppose I'll never get the
chance now, but I hope one day if by
chance he happens to read this poem, then
he'll know that it's for him. For that afternoon
when the summer sun was beating down
and breaking in through the bedroom window.

WHEN I WANT TO WRITE A LOVE POEM

CONTINUATION

WHEN I WANT TO WRITE A LOVE POEM

OUR UNSPOKEN VOW

There's something about the way your fingertips feel on my skin that settles my nerves each time we lie here in the dark. Something about the way you outline my imperfections and place kisses on my scars that makes it easy for me to fall in love even when I don't mean to. As we lie here wrapped in sheets there is no need for words, in this embrace, as worlds collide, in each touch – new language is spoken. We breathe in whispers of desire, and break our unspoken vow that this will be the last time.

I THINK IT'S HIS EYES

I think it's his eyes that make
me want to surrender myself to
him, something about how they
hold me in their grasp, even
when they're looking at me through
a camera's lens. It's an old photo,
but it's one that my mind likes
to remind me of even on days when
I'm not trying to think about him.
I love it and I hate it at the same time,
I love and hate him at the same time.
The way he can control me with a
single glance, the way a slight shift in
tone or even a well-timed silence can
make me crumble inwards and come
alive again in shivers. I don't even
think he realises the effect he has on
me, but how do I even begin telling him?

IN THE DARK

I love the late nights when I
get to lie there in the dark, unable
to see but feeling him close. The
way his breath feels on my skin,
the feel of his body lying next to
mine and the way I impulsively
react when he kisses me or moves
in closer. I love when he bites my
lip and I let out a heavy exhale, he
knows that in this moment – I am his.
When he kisses my neck and I feel
him push himself into me, when I
surrender control and give in to
compulsion. I gasp and he sees the
evil smile appear on my face that he's
been waiting for. He loves it.

AN UNREQUITED LOVE AFFAIR

Loving you is like a one-sided love
affair – when you go home, you go home
and forget about me until next time,
whereas I will go on replaying every
second of our time together like a black
and white silent movie in my head. You
are my unrequited love affair, the habit I
know I should stop before I get hurt but
don't. I think River Song put it best, in
her speech about how you never expect a
sunset to admire you back. That is how
I think of you. I am like River and you are
The Doctor, you're off doing whatever
the hell you want and not giving a damn
about me, and I'm just fine with that.

PASSENGER SEAT

There's something about sitting here, passenger side, with you gripping tight on the wheel, that gets my gets my heart racing. Something about hearing the music playing in the background as I watch the glow of the traffic lights pass us by that makes me impatient. Will your grip on me be that tight? As we race through the backstreets my mind wanders. Thinking back on previous car rides, how they ended, I watch you drive us around as I run my fingers through my hair and think about how this car ride is going to end. Will you make my head spin? Will you make me shake like thunder. Will you inject my skeleton with the lightning in your fingertips and bring me back to life? As we pull up outside the darkened house, my heartbeat drum plays so loud that I'm surprised you can't hear it.

HAVEN'T SPOKEN FOR MONTHS

We haven't spoken since the
last time you came round, there's so
much I want to tell you but then I
see that you've been online for hours
and realise that if you wanted to talk
then you would have messaged me. I
see the Snapchat icon in my notifications
and my mind and heart race as if in
competition with each other only to
crash into a brick wall when my eyes
tell them that it wasn't you. That instead
of a message from you, Snapchat was
telling me about people I may know
but have never heard of. We haven't
spoken since the last time you came
round – and what a night that was.

UNATTACHED

We were only supposed to be a one-time thing all those years ago as we kissed under the tinsel in the bus station. We were never supposed to happen again, but who'd have thought that childish bet we made about when I turned 16 would become the reason why I drink vodka on Bonfire Night to remember the time when I was 19 and we went for a late-night drive. We weren't supposed to be anything, no emotions, no feelings, no attachment to each other, and I suppose we still work that way. We are late-night conversations, adrenaline filled notifications, we are secret kisses and heavy breathing, you're the longest relationship that I've never been in. There was never an identifiable first date, no update to relationship status on Facebook, no giving me a hoodie or one of your shirts to sleep in, but this way works better for us. We are unexclusive, unattached, we are no more than whispers in the dark, but most of the time, I wouldn't change a thing.

TATTOOS & TEMPTATION

To me, you are tattoos and
temptation, an invisible ink that
is etched onto my skin, you're
always there, you'll always be there,
like a stain, a memory that I can
no longer erase, but only I
can see you. Only I can see your
faded markings, the burning red
of my skin after you've left your mark
once again.

IX XII XXI

Whenever I think back on that
night, whenever I think back on our
skeletons intertwined and our flesh
pressed together, I think about how
your fingertips on my spine felt like I
was being injected with lightning —
you brought me back to life. When you
asked me if I was okay — if I was sure —
I knew that it was safe to surrender. The
tension I'd been clinging to had gone
and I felt myself melt into your embrace.
We had no conductor but together we
found our own rhythm. Your hands
played my ribs like piano keys, lifting me
higher and higher until only the angels
could hear me sing. With eyes closed
I was still able to read your every note
and even when we got lost between the
sheets we were able to find our way
again. We improvised. We experimented.
Tried new chords. New melodies. Together
in the darkness of the intrusive streetlamp
light outside the bedroom window —
together we composed music of a new
genre. A genre with the adrenaline of Jazz
but the softness of Blues, something
classical and timeless and yet completely
brand new, something just for us. That
night became my favourite song and I listen
to it again and again — when I'm accompanied
by intrusive streetlamps or when I
hear a G on piano, I think of you.

THE NIGHT AFTER

There's something about the night
after he's been that keeps my mind
racing, something about lying in the
same sheets, surrounded by the smell
of sweat and the echoes of hours
spent panting. He's no longer here but
the grazing of his nails in my skin still
feels present. I close my eyes and I still
see him lying there in the dark - eyes
luminous as moonlight breaks in through
the bedroom window. The bed is still
warm. I can still feel his fingers in my hair.
I can still taste him on my lips. It's now
been two days since I last saw him but it
still feels like five minutes ago.

LATE NIGHT CONVERSATIONS

Late night conversations, whispers in the dark, tell me, if our words came out in daylight, how many worlds would we tear apart? If our private orchestras became sold out concerts, and our symphonies were played out loud for all to hear, would you stay? Right now, we co-exist as two ships passing in the night, and even though you leaving makes me sad I know that the world is round and our paths will cross again one day. But the wait is killing me. I'm drowning and I want you to save me.

BAD HABITS

Some nights I feel like you
would be harder to give
up than cigarettes or alcohol.
You're an addiction like
any other, designed to get
me out of my head, to take
a breather, to destress, but
each time I see the grin on
your face as you watch me
undress, I realise that this
works both ways. We are
each other's bad habits, I am
your nicotine and you are my
bottle of vodka, there are no
patches or meetings for this
kind of relief, but even if
there were, I'd rather we used
each other. You're the bad
habit I'm not ready to give up
despite the long list of
friends who are always telling
me that I should if you're
my bottle of vodka then I'd
rather never be sober.

WHEN I WANT TO WRITE A LOVE POEM

"You've got a fast car, is it fast enough that
we can fly away?"
- Fast Car, Tracy Chapman

When I want to write a love poem,
I listen to the song that reminds
me of you and think about how within
seconds my eyes are closed and my
hips are swaying from side to side
to the sad guitar of the opening verse.
I sing silently into the night. I drink
vodka. I dance around my room in the
dark with the ghost of you — and when
the beat hits, when the drums awaken
the adrenaline in me at 1am when I can't
sleep, I'm reminded of the adrenaline I
had during that teenage first kiss — or a
few years later, on the night we went for a
drive — or the night we wrote our own
genres by the invasive streetlamp light —
or the birthday you offered to pick me up
to go for a drive at 11 o'clock at night. You're
the song that I can't get out of my head,
you are my sad guitar, my soft beating drum
that comes alive for the chorus, my grand piano.

I WISH YOU CAME WITH A WARNING

I wish you came with a warning,
not a label I could ignore, not a backstreet
whisper that I could tell myself I'd
misheard, but a big flashing red light. I
wish I knew of your cyanide kisses before
that afternoon over Christmas, wish I
knew that the lightning in your fingertips
wasn't love, or lust, something I could
live with, but instead was just the
beginning of the storm that I was standing
too close to, to see.

TRUTH OR DARE?

Do you remember the night
we played truth or dare? It is a
night that no matter how hard
I try, I just can't make myself
forget it. The night we played
truth or dare was the night I told
you about her like it was a good
idea. A stroke of genius that
became more of a moment of
madness. It was a confession that
I regret making. The night I told
you about my first sad guitar or
my first violin and the nights would
spend watching movies together,
was the day I threw you into her
arms and gave you the excuse
to forget about me.

WHEN I WANT TO WRITE A LOVE POEM

DETERIORATION

WHEN I WANT TO WRITE A LOVE POEM

THE NIGHT SHE WAS THERE

"GIRL'S LOVE, GIRLS AND BOYS."
- GIRLS/GIRLS/BOYS, PANIC! AT THE DISCO

The night that she was there, was full
of twists and turns and panting as the
3 of us made music together. Legs
tangled and wrapped in sheets we didn't
know what we were doing only that we were
having fun. The night I learned to play a
harmonica and a violin at the same time,
was the night I caressed her curves and
felt his strings press up against me. It was
the first time I'd felt completely like myself
while at the same time feeling completely
afraid. What if they didn't like my music?
What if he preferred her melodies to mine?
What if she only agreed because she wanted
to hear how he strums his guitar? In the
end I took the role of quiet piano while she
became an electric bass. I was still a part
of the song but somewhere after the chorus
I'd managed to fade into the background.

THE FIRST VIOLIN

> "WE'RE NOT LOVERS, WE'RE JUST STRANGERS WITH THE SAME DAMN HUNGER TO BE TOUCHED, TO BE LOVED, TO FEEL ANYTHING AT ALL."
> - STRANGERS, HALSEY (FEAT. LAUREN JAUREGUI)

The first time I felt the curves of
a violin - I was 14 years old and
having a sleepover at a friend's house.
I remember the quiet music that we
made as her parents slept in the next
room - a symphony that became a
heart break anthem as she later told me
that she preferred him instead of me.
I can still remember the rush I felt on
that first walk of shame as I made my
way home still drunk on our melodies –
the way her singing stayed with me
when she was long out of reach. The day
she told me about him, was the day I
realised that it had all been a lie. That she
didn't like my music, but just wanted to
tell him that she'd been to the concert.
That night wasn't a heartfelt hymn,
but a rehearsal for when she later
played her music with him.

SECRET SYMPHONY

She was my secret symphony, she was the quiet band practice in the basement where we sang of nights spent drinking gin. She could have been my biggest hit, my greatest achievement, my symphony that would be heard even long after I'm gone, but I was so afraid of the crowd's reaction that she never got published. She became the song I'd listen to with quiet headphones when I thought know one was around, and for that I'm sorry. She deserved so much better, she deserved to be a sold out concert played daily on the radio, not hidden away from the crowd.

NO MORE SCATTERED NIGHTS, PLEASE?

Tonight, can we just watch
movies? Bring a blanket downstairs
and curl up together on the sofa?
If we watch Disney, then I promise
to try and not sing along with each
lyric that is played, and if you could run
your fingers through my hair then I
promise to try and stay awake. When I
ask you to come round, I'm not always
looking for lighting, and I've tried to
tell you that a million times but you
never seem to hear me, so I thought
I'd try something different and write
a poem that you'll never read because
well, why would you? So tonight, can
we just watch movies? Can we pretend
to be a normal couple for just one night
before going back to being strangers
who rely on scattered nights.

HOME BY MIDNIGHT

There's something about being told
to be home by midnight that only
adds to the false fairytale that I play
in my head whenever I hear your engine
running outside. Something about
the word 'midnight' that makes me
think of your car as a pumpkin
that you stole from a local patch and
must soon return before it's too late.
But like with Cinderella's night at the
ball I know that this is only temporary.
That soon you'll forget what I looked
like, forget the dress, forget the hair, the
makeup, and try every girl in the village
before you eventually circle back to
me. Each time I ask myself why I
do it, why I bother, why I do this to
myself again and again, but like in my
least favourite fairy tale, the princess
still married the prince who couldn't
recognise the girl he supposedly loved
until she tried on the glass slipper.

A DIFFERENT KIND OF ADRENALINE

Tonight, was a different kind of adrenaline - the kind made of soft touches and gentle kisses that make my knees go weak, the kind that makes my head spin in all the right ways. Tonight, there was no lightning just quiet thunder - the kind that makes you want to hold someone closer, feel their warm body pressed up against you. His fingertips on my skin were what I didn't know I needed until I felt him trace all of my imperfections until I felt good about them. Now I am no longer afraid of my scars but I'm in love with them – and I will continue to love them.

WHAT WOULD WE BE LIKE?

What would we be like? If we were
no longer reliant on scattered nights,
would we be days, weeks, months,
would we be years? I hope so. I hope
we would be the couple that people
would look at and smile, I hope we'd
be the couple that got to grow old
together. Would we be albums filled
with faded photos, yes. I'd like that. I'd
like to one day wake up years from now,
roll over and see you sleeping next to
me. It sounds like such a nice dream.

GRAND PIANO

I used to call you my grand piano
because I felt that with you, I could
become anything. Every song, no
matter the genre, all start with the
gentle pressing of piano keys – a
simple melody could become either
an adrenaline filled jazz classic or a soft
blues lullaby, and with you I feel like
I too could become either. You played
my ribs like piano keys, lifting me higher
and higher, you taught me notes I
never thought it was possible to reach –
and I think about that night often.
About the glow of the invasive
streetlamp light and the smile on my
face the next day that stretched from
ear to ear.

HE LIKED MY POETRY

He liked my poetry. I wasn't expecting him to - I didn't think he'd read them, never mind like them. I was shy to show him at first, shy to let him see the hold he has on me, shy to let him see how I think about him enough to write poems about our scattered nights together. I couldn't explain it to him then, not in a way he'd understand, but even though his fingertips have explored every inch of my skin, even though our skeletons have been intertwined and he's touched all of my scars – poetry is a lot more personal to me than that. Poetry is what is being said between heavy breaths when we can barely stand to keep our lips apart, it's the music we make when we're lost between the sheets: it's the rushing to get dressed afterwards like a pair of teenagers not wanting to get caught.

THE DAY I SAW YOU IN TOWN WITH HER

The day I saw you in town with
her, was the beginning of the end
for us. As I saw you from across the
roundabout walking back to either
your place or hers, it was the moment
I realised that my deepest fears had
come true and that you preferred
her melodies to mine. Decided that
you would rather learn how to play her
electric base than continue to make music
with my piano keys, rather them fade and
grow out of tune than putting in the
time to retune them again. I tried to call
while I saw you both walking together,
heard the familiar ringtone in the distance
and watched as you hung up the phone.
I could have easily walked faster and caught
up to you both, called you out then and
there, but instead, I went home alone.

TERMINATION

WHEN I WANT TO WRITE A LOVE POEM

THEIR SONG

As his footsteps can be heard
coming slowly up the stairs, the
adrenaline kicks in and her heart
begins to beat the rhythm of their
new song. Slowly at first. They are
their own instruments but each time
they play — the chords get thrown
around and jumbled up and each
time they are played in a different
order — a chorus becomes a verse,
the bridge becomes the intro, the
pre-chorus graduates to chorus,
but the outro always remains the same.
This time, their song began with the
gentle crashing of cymbals, and soon
the gentle fingering of piano keys,
together they exchanged oxygen and
breathed life into each other the way
a performer would his saxophone.
Her curves are his glass violin as he
plays the most beautiful music while
trying not to break her. When the chorus
hits, her heartbeat drum is racing, sweat,
panting, dancing to their new song,
this room is their stage, and they are the
performers and the audience
rolled up into one.

WHEN YOU READ MY POETRY

When you first read my poetry, I
couldn't even begin to tell you how
nervous I was. I couldn't describe
the feeling in my chest when a notification
told me that you'd read them. I'm still
not sure what to think. Your response
was so vague, I told you I loved you
but you were too caught up in saying
that you couldn't believe that someone
would write you poetry. That should
have told me that it was the end.

I STILL HAVE THE BOTTLE OF VODKA

I don't know why I kept it, perhaps
I was inspired by that scene in Friends
when Rachel shows Ross the box of
trinkets that she's saved over the years.
Perhaps it's because I used to scrapbook
and would always save little mementos
because it could be a cute anniversary gift
idea, full of photos and cinema tickets
and the card he got me for Valentine's Day.
I still have the bottle of vodka from our
first night together, black labelled with
Russian writing, tucked away in the back
of the bottom draw. It's been empty for
years, I don't know why I kept it, we'll never
have an anniversary. There'll never be a
Valentine's Day dinner or Christmas with
the in-laws, but I think that's why I love
him so much. I think that's why I kept the
bottle of vodka after all these years. With
him there was never any pressure, with him
I never felt compelled to do anything
more than sing.

WE WERE NEVER ROMEO & JULIET

We have never been a Romeo and Juliet kind of love story, have we? Sure there have been things keeping us apart, sure at one point I probably would have died for you, but there was always Rosaline – watching, waiting, lurking in the shadows. We never had a balcony scene either, or even if we did it was probably the other way around where you waited on the balcony and I observed from down below. You seemed to always have the higher ground, even when you were wrong, but I fell for it all because I thought that you were the one, that this was it, but then again, there was always Rosaline.

ONE LAST NIGHT

If you must leave, can we have
one last night together? Can we have
one last night of adrenaline filled lightning
that melts into quiet thunder? A night
full of twists and turns, panting and
dancing, let tonight be our swan-song
as we make music under the starlight. Let's
make a night to remember, something for
us both to look back on when we're in bed
lying next to sleeping lovers, the kind of
night we compare our futures to, the kind
of night that stays with us even when we're
old and grey. Let's play our genre, dust
off our piano keys and see what happens
when we mix the adrenaline of Jazz with the
softness of blues. Let's enjoy one last night
together surrounded by my favourite song.

WE WERE GONNA BE TIMELESS

We were gonna be timeless you
and I, in a dream once, you said as
much yourself. But as the clock struck
one on that cold summer night, the
ending drew nearer as you kissed me
goodbye. I wasn't surprised though, as
the words left your lips. Ever since that
afternoon it has only been a matter of
time. The clock tick, tick ticking as the
days went by. Pretending like I didn't
know that it was coming, acting stupid,
feeling worse, pretending that I was trying
to make the most of what days I had
left when in reality I only stayed because
I was afraid of being alone. I wasn't ready
to say goodbye to you yet. I wasn't ready
to accept that everything we could have
been was all a distant dream.

LAST KISS

I never thought we'd have a last
kiss, you were the one that I thought
was going to last forever, so when it
did happen, when you kissed me
goodbye for the final time before
going to be with her, it hurt. Even
though I knew it was coming. Even
though I'd been counting down the
days since that afternoon when I
saw you in town together. It still came
as a surprise when it finally happened.

MESSAGE NOT DELIVERED

Hey.
Message not delivered.

I'm sorry that it's late, but I saw the time and thought of you.
Message not delivered.

It hurt; you know.
Message not delivered.

The day you walked out.
Message not delivered.

I know it's been a while, but it still hurts.
Message not delivered.

I just can't forget what you did.
Message not delivered.

I try.
Message not delivered.

I've tried everything.
Message not delivered.

I'm sorry, I'll stop.
Message not delivered.

I'll leave you in peace.
Message not delivered.

I love you.
Message not delivered.

Goodbye.
Message delivered.

WHEN I WANT TO WRITE A LOVE POEM

Hello?
Message received.

A POET IN LOVE

You let a poet fall in love with you
on that night all those years ago, how
could you be so selfish? I wrote you
poems when our tongues were tied,
I made you immortal with my words.
When we are both nothing but dust the
poems I wrote you will still be sitting
on someone's shelves, covered in particles
of us, but what have you given in return?
Scattered nights of broken maybes, the
inspiration to write poems, an unrequited
love affair. You kissed a poet in the
dark and sat back and watched as I fell
in love and fell apart. You let a poet
fall in love with you, how could you be
so cruel?

WHEN I WANT TO WRITE A LOVE POEM (REPRISED)

> "YOU'VE GOT A FAST CAR, IS IT FAST ENOUGH SO YOU CAN FLY AWAY?"
> - FAST CAR, TRACY CHAPMAN

When I want to write a love poem,
I listen to the song that reminds me of
you and think about how I let you
keep me a secret for years and I was
completely okay with it. If it was anyone
else, I know I wouldn't have been, if
you were anyone else then I wouldn't
have called the red flags that I saw every
time your name popped up on my phone
screen as green light. I should have
listened to my friends, should have quit
the bad habit that for all this time has
been holding me back, but when I see
your grin, when I feel the adrenaline,
I forget their advice and I fall in love
all over again. But now when I listen to
the song that reminds me of you, instead
of drinking vodka and thinking about
late night car rides, I'll drink whiskey and
think of late nights spent at a pool bar
with my friends. I no longer dance around
in the dark with the ghost of you, but
instead when the beat hits, when the drums
awaken the adrenaline in me at 1am when I
can't sleep, I'm reminded of the adrenaline

WHEN I WANT TO WRITE A LOVE POEM

that I felt when my book got published,
or the time I saw My Chemical Romance
live, or the way it felt after graduation or
the applause I get after reading out a poem
at an open mic. You're no longer stuck in
my head. I learned new songs. I learned
to live without you and to make my own music.

MOVING ON

WHEN I WANT TO WRITE A LOVE POEM

THE HIGHS & LOWS OF HEARTBREAK

He messaged so I'm high on life
again, but I know that it will soon
be over, I wish I could quit him,
quit this, I wish I could get off this
roller coaster. When I'm high I'm
in the heavens, singing loudly with
the music we make, but when the
lows hit; I know it's a matter of time
before I'm destined to break. But
how do I quit this bad habit, how do
I erase his touch from my skin, how
do I forget the nights we spent together,
his blue eyes and subtle grin.

PINTEREST BOARDS & NURSERY WALLS

I had my future planned out with you, there was a comfortable feeling of certainty embedded in the Pinterest boards that I'd spent my days building of my future and what it would look like – a section for DIY wedding favours, another for the colour schemes of our children's nursery, a third for what our home would look like. I think I asked you once, what your dream wedding would be, you said you wanted a small service in the glow of moonlight – I suppose that's why it hurt so much when you said goodbye in the middle of the night.

DANCING ON MY OWN

The first time I went dancing
on my own, I hated every second
of it because it didn't feel like you.
No matter what I did, no matter
how hard I tried; I couldn't make
myself sing in the way that you did.
My piano keys were out of tune, the
wax to my violin bow had all grown
dry. That night I didn't make music,
just fragments of broken song. So I
decided to find myself a new conductor,
someone who would retune my piano
keys by ear, someone who knew the
music that they were capable of making,
but instead of the expert I was promised,
he was nothing more than an amateur,
an actor, someone who had never before
felt the curves of a violin never mind
know how to play one.

DO YOUR SYMPHONIES SOUND LIKE OURS?

When you play her on your guitar,
or when you listen to her sing your songs,
does she remind you of how we used
to dance? Do her melodies make you
think of me? Do her piano keys remind
you of our valentine's night and the
black and white vintage dress that I was
wearing? Do I ever cross your mind
when you're kissing her, caressing her
violin curves, when you lie her down
between your sheets of jumbled up chords,
does she ever make you think of me? Probably
not. I am the quiet piano in the background
of one of your greatest hits while she is
the saxophone, loud, proud, front and
centre — drowning out my melodies
with her excitement.

YOU'LL BE CRYING OVER ME

One day, I don't know when, but
one day in the future, I'll catch you
looking at photos of us and I'll see
you crying. I don't know how I'm going
to feel that day, sad because I too will
miss the memories, happy because you've
finally realised what it was that you gave
up when you chose her. One day you'll
look back on the day we went roller
skating, or the afternoons we'd spend
in the milkshake bar, or the mornings
I'd come round early, or the nights when
I'd stay out late. One day in the future,
you'll be crying over me, and I can finally
say that I'm not sorry.

LOSING YOU

Losing you was the hardest thing
that I've ever had to do. Before you left
my world was viewed through rose
tinted lenses which made even
the most beautiful sunsets look
like a colourless sky. I remodelled
myself to be with you, lost parts of
who I am, gave you the parts of me that I'd
been saving and left nothing for myself.
After you left, it took me a while,
but I've finally found who I am again.
I'm Ember, I'm a writer, a poet,
a photographer, proud dog parent to a
spaniel named Oliver. I like to cook,
spend time with friends, watch movies,
I watch cartoons after watching
a horror movie because I know I won't
sleep otherwise. I'm me.

LOVING MYSELF

I'm loving myself now. I don't
need you anymore. I know I should
have probably done this first, but
I was so swept away, that I didn't
have time to learn how. But I'm
learning now. I'm learning to tune
my own piano keys by ear, learning
to understand what I need to do for
the music to be just right. I'm writing
my own melodies now, learning to freestyle
and go with the flow of the music.
I taught myself so that I no longer
need to rely on a conductor. Maybe
one day I'll show you the symphonies
that I've become, perhaps one day
I'll thank you for getting me started
and showing me the chords to play.

PROGRESS

For me, progress is forgetting
the words to a song that I used to
listen to religiously. Every couple
has a song and ours was framed
on top of the wardrobe. Today I
was talking to someone about the
artist behind that song, and I was
about to say the name of my favourite
and I couldn't remember what it was
called or how it goes. For most people
this would be the most stressful
experience, to have a song in your
head that you can't remember, but
for me, for me this is progress. When
my greatest strength is my memory for
lyrics and I forget the song that
reminds me of you, this is progress.
You're fading. Finally. After all this time.

I DON'T LOVE YOU

"I DON'T LOVE YOU, LIKE I DID, YESTERDAY."
I DON'T LOVE YOU, MY CHEMICAL ROMANCE.

I don't love you anymore. I don't
love you anymore. I don't love you
anymore. With each passing day the
poetry gets harder to write, as I can no
longer hear our genre playing on a loop
in the back of my mind. I dust off my
keyboard and play a G note but instead
of you, all I think about is standing in a
crowd screaming, singing, cheering, dancing,
dressed in black and celebrating a teenage
dream coming true. You're no longer the
first song that I play when I wake up in the
morning, or the evening melody that sings
me to sleep. I don't love you anymore.

GOODBYE SAD GUITAR

"I WANNA SAY 'I WISH THAT YOU NEVER LEFT' BUT INSTEAD 'I ONLY WISH YOU THE BEST'"
- WISH YOU THE BEST, LEWIS CAPALDI

I hope your private symphonies become sold out concerts. I hope that one day everyone gets to hear the music that it took you both so long to make. I hope that after all this time she doesn't become your campo, restricting your sound into the way that she wants it, but instead I hope she writes you songs that you can learn how to play. I hope she gives you a happy melody, for so long now I've only heard you play the saddest of songs. I hope she teaches you to play in a major key. I hope you tell her Te Amo in between the chorus and the verse. I hope she gives you new strings for your guitar, an opportunity for you to start again.

ABOUT THE AUTHOR

Ember Birchall is a writer and poet who uses their surroundings and experiences as an influence for their work. They have a Bachelor of Arts in English Literature and Creative Writing from Staffordshire University and a passion for exploring their hometown as well as favourite travel locations through poetry, prose, and photography. They live in Warrington, UK with their family and four dogs, Teddy, Tula, Oliver, and Paddy. You can find more of their work on Amazon or by following them on TikTok @loverofwordsandrhyme.

Printed in Great Britain
by Amazon

37506091R00050